Career F

G000149297

Praise for John Lees' Work and Careers Books

'John Lees is one of the grand masters in the burgeoning field of careers coaching. His practical yet inspiring approach helps people not only to make the right career decisions but to work out how they can live their lives to the full, and with meaning.'
Liz Hall, Editor, Coaching at Work

'John Lees is brilliant at creating the kind of mind shift we all need to see ourselves and our work in a way that lets us trans- form both.'
Maureen Rice, Editor, Psychologies

'I know first hand the joy that being in the right career can bring and I commend John Lees for his books and seminars which help other people do just that.'
Rosemary Conley CBE

'John Lees' work is both inspirational and motivational, urging you to constantly think outside the box. He challenges you to lose the excuses and to take managing your career into your own hands.'
Sarah Kenyon, Career Development Specialist, Orange

'No matter how many barriers – real or imagined – are currently preventing you making the career change you know you need, this book will help you demolish them more effectively than a wrecking ball. John's books are thought-provoking, stimulating, challenging and a pleasure to read – and this is no exception. It could well change your life.'
Steve Crabb, Editor, People Management

Career Reboot

24 tips for tough times

JOHN LEES

Career Reboot
John Lees
ISBN 13: 978-0-07-712758-9
ISBN 10: 0-07-712758-7

 **Professional**

Published by:
McGraw-Hill Publishing Company
Shoppenhangers Road, Maidenhead, Berkshire, England, SL6 2QL
Telephone: 44 (0) 1628 502500
Fax: 44 (0) 1628 770224
Website: www.mcgraw-hill.co.uk

British Library Cataloguing in Publication Data
A catalogue record of this book is available from the British Library.

McGraw-Hill books are great for training, as gifts, and for
promotions. Please contact our corporate sales executive to
discuss special quantity discounts or customisation to support
your initiatives: b2b@mcgraw-hill.com.

Typeset by RefineCatch Limited, Bungay, Suffolk
Printed in Great Britain by Bell and Bain Ltd, Glasgow

Mixed Sources
Product group from well-managed
forests and other controlled sources
www.fsc.org Cert no. TT-COC-002769
© 1996 Forest Stewardship Council

The McGraw·Hill Companies

About the author

John Lees is one of the UK's best known career coaches and authors. *How To Get A Job You'll Love* has twice been WH Smith's 'Business Book of the Month', and regularly tops the list as the best-selling careers book by a British author.

John specialises in helping people make difficult career decisions – difficult because they don't know what to do next, or because there are barriers in the way of success. He has delivered workshops in the USA, South Africa, Australia and New Zealand and regularly speaks at UK events (Forum3, One Life Live) and has also featured as a speaker at the world's largest international career conferences in the USA.

He writes regularly for *The Times*, *The Guardian*, and has a regular column in People Management. His work has been featured on the Channel 4 *Dispatches* programme and in the BBC Interactive *Back to Work* programme, and he regularly provides insights into the world of work on radio and in publications including *Management Today*, *The Sunday Times*, *Daily Express*, *Daily Mirror*, *Psychologies*, *Eve* and *She*.

John is a graduate of the universities of Cambridge, London and Liverpool and has spent most of his career focusing on the world of work. He has trained recruitment specialists since the mid-1980s, and is the former Chief Executive of the Institute of Employment Consultants (now the Recruitment & Employment Confederation, REC). He now runs a careers consultancy in the North West of the UK.

John Lees Associates provides one-to-one career coaching in most parts of the UK. For details email info@johnleescareers.com or visit www.johnlees careers.com.

Contents

Contents

How this book will help you

This book is designed to help you get out of a hole, quickly, if you're career-panicked, especially if you're coping with redundancy. All the chapters in **Section 1 – Taking Stock** (Chapters 1-5) need to be read together before you begin any kind of organised job search. **Section 2 – Planning Your Strategy** (Chapters 6-11), gives you insights into the way the market works and the way recruiters and employers react to the different behaviours adopted by job seekers. **Section 3 – Your Message To The Marketplace** (Chapters 12-16) provides a series of checklists to show you how to sell yourself on paper, and **Section 4 – Interview Secrets** (Chapters 17-20) reveals how to make an impact in the final stages of the selection process. Finally, because your new career begins here, **Section 5 – Looking Forward** (Chapters 21-24) provides some longer-term strategies and thinking.

SECTION ONE
Taking stock

1

Get a grip – focus on what's working, not what isn't

You may be reading this book because your job faces an uncertain future, or you've been made redundant. You're worried about finding something else – you're job hunting and you've had disappointing results.

It's easy to be confused by recruiter feedback or put off by rejection. Worse still, you may have been panicked into feeling that nothing will work.

Before you take another step, focus on what's working, not what's going wrong. How many of the roles you have applied for have been centre target? Random applications for roles where you're unlikely to get shortlisted often result in rejection, and unless you're careful this can lead to a loss of confidence. It's pointless considering wild shots as failures.

Concentrate on the results you achieve applying for jobs you want and might get.

- Trainee pilots are taught to face emergencies by not putting their focus on what is broken, but on whatever is still working enough to get you safely on the ground. Looking just at the downside of job search will ultimately drag down your performance. Look carefully at the results you are getting from your job search. Where have you received genuine feedback? What needs fixing?

- Seek independent advice from anyone with recruitment or HR experience before you send out your CV – does it say what you want it to say?

- Don't just dash off a poorly revised CV. Average paperwork gets you average results. How clearly have you presented your personal strengths? What have you done to stand out from the crowd on paper?

- Don't ask recruiters what they think of your CV. Ask them *what your CV says*. If you recognise and can make sense of what you hear, your CV is working.

- Get focused on the fact that you will be making *claims* and offering *evidence* in communications: work out what you're good at *and* where you've done it.

- Perform a quick career review. What are your career highlights? What have you done well? What would you do differently in the future? What motivates you?

- Don't dwell on unhappy interviews. Ask for advice about what you could do better, not about why you failed to get the job. Look at what has gone well, and how you can build on it.

- Don't be over-influenced by views of the job market from friends and relatives – their picture is probably inaccurate.

- Keep your confidence up by putting on smart business clothes at least once a week and having face-to-face conversations, even if it's just with friends or colleagues.

Thinking yourself into a corner is the best way of limiting your options. Focus on what's out there, not what's missing.

2

Practical steps to keep your head above water

Moving forward isn't just about your job search. You need to take stock and look at practical considerations. Dealing with what is really going on in your life and the practical consequences will help you see beyond panic mode and allow you to do some long-term planning. Worrying just about the things you need to worry about will help clear your mind for the next stage in your career. A few practical steps will help put you in the right frame of mind.

After redundancy, take advice to make sure you are being treated reasonably fairly. This doesn't mean getting bogged down in a battle with your employer or arguing about why your job has been cut – both are a great waste of time and energy. However, do ensure that you understand everything about the process you're going through.

- Make sure you know your legal rights – how you should be treated, your notice period, and whether you will receive a redundancy payment.

- Your trade union or professional body may be able to offer advice about correct procedures, and what to do if your employer is insolvent. Your local Citizens Advice Bureau can also offer help.

- Ask for all contractual details in writing – and your P45 – before you leave.

- Find out if your present employer can help – for example, a CV review, practice interviews, or introductions to agencies or other employers.

- Ask about any benefits you might retain if you are a member of an employer pension scheme.

- Look closely at the impact of redundancy on your lifestyle, your finances, and your career options. Work out how long you can afford to live on your savings, redundancy payment and any other income you receive.

- Get organised – collect the information you will need to rewrite your CV, including details of recent work duties and training. Ask for time off to look for work before you leave the job.

- Draw up a list of what you need to spend each month on essentials and create a budget for the next 3 months. Cut back on inessentials.

- Find out what state benefits you may be entitled to.

- If you receive a redundancy payment, take professional advice before spending it or saving it somewhere where your funds can't be accessed in a hurry.

- Cut back where you can – but not on the travel required to go to interviews or to meet people to talk about work opportunities.

- Smarten up your wardrobe – clean, repair, buy or borrow so you look the part if you go anywhere near a decision maker.

Don't panic – many have travelled this way before. Take stock before you rush at the job market.

3

Timing things sensibly

When redundancy strikes it's tempting to quickly fire off a hastily adapted CV and start chasing job advertisements. You may want to ring all the agencies you know and start networking. You might get an interview, but it's far more likely that you will blunder into some fairly difficult questions and negative feedback, including the fact that you lack a sense of direction.

Recruiters see these half-hearted applications every week – a hurriedly patched-up CV, an interview candidate who hasn't learned how to talk about leaving the job without a huge amount of emotional baggage, and a complete lack of direction.

Timing your return to the market means finding the right balance between recovery and inertia – move too soon and you send out all the wrong messages, too late and you've lost any sense of energy and missed vital opportunities.

- Don't be pressurised by family or friends into a hasty job search with a poor CV and an unclear message about what you're looking for.

- On the other hand, don't use reflection as an excuse to wait for ever. If there are opportunities in your sights, go for them with the best CV rewrite you can do in a hurry.

- Avoid talking to employers while you still feel bitter or angry about leaving.

- When colleagues or friends cut out 'perfect' job ads for you, thank them and then describe what you are actually looking for.

- Resist advice to 'take any kind of job' – you'll be struggling to explain your CV in 5 years' time if you do so.

- Don't use up opportunities to talk to your best contacts until you have got a clear idea of what you are going to say to them about your future.

- Begin with active research – map the territory before sending out job applications.

- Think about how you spend your time – are you spending enough time actively working on your career options? Are you using a random job search as an excuse not to do some career thinking?

- Include activities in your schedule which have nothing to do with work. A brisk walk or run may improve your spirits more than a pep talk.

- Don't go near a recruiter until you can give a short, upbeat answer to the questions 'Why are you on the market at the moment?' and 'Why did you leave your last job?'

■ Don't phone a decision maker if you're feeling at a low ebb. Wait until you're feeling upbeat, then make the phone call standing up – you'll be more confident and sound more energised.

■ If you're not getting interviews, adjust your aim rather than resetting your goals. Review what you are doing wrong in terms of getting your message across.

Take time to stock your lifeboat before you jump ship.

4

What gets in the way?

There are external factors constraining your choices – the marketplace, declining industries, finding your way in a tough market – but the most powerful barriers are the ones you create for yourself. Be honest with yourself about the phrases that keep you awake at two o'clock in the morning: 'I don't have any achievements' . . . 'None of my skills are transferable' . . . 'I don't interview well', or the 'Yes, but . . .' you hear when you look at an exciting job ad or opportunity. These internalised constraints get in the way of your confidence *and* your message.

Look for your defence mechanisms – the way you justify a favourite strategy, even though you know it isn't working. Blame the economy. Blame agencies. Blame the people who interviewed you so unprofessionally last week. Blamed enough people? Time to take responsibility and make the changes that will start to make things happen.

- Recruit a couple of positive friends to remind you of what you're good at and keep you on track.

- Talk through your evidence with them. How can you make events sound like achievements? What can you say to convince someone why you made various learning and career choices?

- Look at ways you overcame constraints in the past. Many of the barriers in your way now are fences you have climbed or bypassed some time in the past.

- Go through your work history with a supportive colleague. List all those times you made something special happen, added value, or made a difference.

- Reflect on work, study or life experiences when you were an enthusiastic, high-energy version of yourself. What were you doing? Talk about the skills you were using.

- Practise talking about parts of your experience with real enthusiasm – show passion, don't just talk about it in theory.

- Get used to saying the phrase 'I am a person who can . . .' (followed by a skill you use with proficiency and ease).

- If you're angry about the way you have been treated, be careful you don't let anger become the only thing you talk about. Get frustration and disappointment out of your system before you go anywhere near a recruiter. You may get sympathy, but you won't get shortlisted.

- If you hate ringing people cold, don't do it. Ask people for their help in making introductions on your behalf.

- A job search is a work project and needs clear challenges and deadlines, particularly when it comes to making appointments to see people face to face.

- Remember that few people remain unemployed in the long term, particularly if they are flexible and active in their job search.

- Saying 'I can do anything' simply makes you completely undifferentiated. Don't be a job beggar.

Work out where you want to get to. Your toughest job is not to get in the way of your own progress.

5

Get help to bounce back

Redundancy can be a painful and life-altering experience. Employers always say it's the role not the person made redundant, but that's not how it feels to those on the receiving end. It can knock your confidence so much that you become blind to your employability, fail to appreciate your skills, and start believing you have no options.

The first thing many people experience is a sense of disbelief – is this really happening? Next, you may feel a sense of injustice – *why me?* You may feel angry about what you have gone through. It's natural to feel a sense of loss, particularly if you have been in the job a long time. You may feel a sense of failure or rejection.

Don't become one of the minority of people who never really move on after redundancy. Instead, look at the people who successfully manage transition, and learn from them.

- Talk to people who have been made redundant in the last 2 years and have found work. Learn from their tips and their mistakes.

- Start with the building blocks of a great interview performance. Review your work experience and list *all* your skills and achievements (with a view to editing this information later).

- Think positively: this might be an opportunity to take up a learning opportunity or take stock of what kind of work you enjoy doing.

- Ask anyone you know with recruitment experience about what kind of CV you will need to achieve your goals.

- Don't be afraid to ask your employer for names of useful contacts.

- Draw up a list of the people you have worked with over the last 5 years including colleagues, clients, suppliers and professionals. Talk to as many of them as you can – ideally face to face so that you're remembered.

- Set up a book or worksheet recording your enquiries, contacts and connections. Keep it close by in case you get a phone call from someone you're trying to reach.

- Recruit two good friends to keep you positive, remind you of successful outcomes in your career, and encourage good connections.

- Ask an honest friend to give you tough feedback

on whether your clothes, grooming and haircut are likely to impress at interview.

■ Don't be put off by early rejection – you'll have to hear 'no' several times during your job search, so get used to people not taking your call even at this stage of the game.

■ If others have been laid off at the same time as you, work together to share strategies and to encourage each other to keep looking.

■ Put the same hours into finding a job as you normally put into work, but don't neglect your social life – you'll get support and ideas from people you meet.

After redundancy, get help to rediscover your talents – very few people can do so on their own.

SECTION TWO
Planning your strategy

6

Think multi-strategy

When candidates get 'stuck' in their job search or find that they are getting only rejection letters, there are two usual reasons. The first is that you're not being clear about what you have to offer. The second likely reason is that you are focusing on just one or two job search methods. Internet-based job search is favoured because it's easy, convenient, and there seem to be thousands of vacancies available. A great deal of time is spent registering on Job Boards and sending out electronic applications, followed by . . . silence.

The next favourite methods are to apply for the odd, rare, advertised position and to register with agencies. Here again the wrong overall message will quickly get you sidelined, but at least these methods look and feel like activity.

A multi-strategy approach shortens the odds considerably.

- Use ALL the main job search methods at the same time:

  ✔ Look in newspapers and other publications including specialist and trade press for vacancies.

  ✔ Register with a range of relevant employment agencies, and talk to them in person, ideally face to face.

  ✔ Send your CV out speculatively with a good cover letter to named senior contacts at employers you would like to work for, even if nothing is advertised.

  ✔ Use the Internet to identify target organisations and employer job boards.

  ✔ Scrutinise all job ads, whether paper or electronic, to identify likely employers and useful agencies.

  ✔ Talk to people who have good industry knowledge to ask advice about the best method of approach.

  ✔ Keep your eyes and ears open for opportunities in your local area.

  ✔ Seek face-to-face meetings with people who are working in sectors you find interesting – ask questions about what's happening rather than trying to sell yourself at this stage.

  ✔ In some sectors over 50% of jobs are filled by word of mouth, so ask friends, family, ex-employers, colleagues and social contacts for useful connections and ideas.

✓ Renew contacts with former employers, clients, customers and colleagues. Take them for coffee and find out what's happening in their sector.

✓ Consider appropriate voluntary work experience.

✓ Ask for interview advice from any colleagues and friends who have recruiting experience.

✓ Temporary work can sometimes enable you to prove your worth to an employer.

■ The reality is that there are a range of methods of finding a job, and in order to shorten your time to target you need to do them all, simultaneously, giving maximum effort to any approach that gets you in front of people rather than screens.

■ Keep focused, and keep looking. Getting through to interview in a competitive market requires luck and commitment as well as preparation.

You are more likely to land a job through a face-to-face conversation, even a random one, than spending all week at your PC.

7

Agencies, consultants, and dead ends

If you need to find work in days rather than weeks or months, you'll need to work with recruitment agencies. They have more leverage than you in terms of getting an employer to commit to a shortlist and then to a hiring decision. They often know the sector well and can, if you ask the right questions, give good feedback on your strategy.

Unfortunately in tough times agencies can also be dead ends. Reported behaviours include a complete lack of response, or worse, the message that you will be perfect for a range of roles followed by no further contact. Feedback from agencies can also be problematic in a downturn – because they are hit first by any recession they tend to react by saying 'there are no jobs out there' when what they mean is that vacancies are being filled by other means.

- Don't waste time by approaching the wrong organisations. Find agencies which are (a) recruiting in your sector (they don't always have to be local) and (b) visibly active in the press and on web sites.

- Understand whom you are dealing with – recruitment agencies aren't allowed to charge you a fee for finding you a job. Other organisations may try to charge you.

- Don't be sidelined by requests to email in your CV or register online – try to talk to real people.

- A good way to speak to a real recruitment consultant is to find a job you are interested in and ring up to ask a detailed or technical question about the role.

- Your aim is to get a conversation, and then to build a warm relationship. Remember that recruitment consultants are driven by people, not paper. Sending CVs electronically has little impact.

- Establish a good working relationship with at least six recruiters in your sector. Make sure they are clear about your 'offer' and your ideal role.

- Remember that recruiters only consult their candidate database if they are bored or desperate. Keep building relationships on the telephone or in person.

- Remember that recruiters don't always share candidates or even vacancies with their colleagues

- don't be frightened of talking to more than one branch or consultant.

■ Don't be afraid to be a (very slight) nuisance – the agency will make a decent fee out of placing you in a job.

■ Ask for feedback on the content, not the style, of your CV.

■ Ask for detailed employer briefings, but also do your own homework – at least an hour on the Internet looking at any organisation that offers you an interview.

Recruitment agencies can fast track you into an interview, but you need to manage how they see you.

8

Work with the market, don't blame it

If you read the press you'll easily believe there are no jobs out there. Bemoaning the state of the market is a great excuse for a low-octane job search. Don't blame it, understand it.

In many sectors the majority of jobs are not advertised. If you only ever respond to job advertisements, you'll never know about them. This is the hidden job market, and most people believe they don't know how to break into it.

If you want reduce your options, then just chase advertised positions. You'll miss out on most newly created jobs, all unadvertised positions filled by word of mouth, and most jobs with small or niche organisations. You'll miss out on all those companies that are just on the edge of thinking about creating a new job. You'll never have a chance to be recommended by a friend or colleague.

- Breaking into the hidden market isn't about old school tie networks or special favours, nor is it only open to those who are great at self-promotion. It's about meeting new people, and making sure they remember just a few positive pieces of information about you.

- The best definition of the hidden job market is *what people say about you when you're not in the room*. Make sure that you leave everyone you meet with a clear picture.

- Getting mentioned isn't a matter of chance. Tell people what you're looking for and what you have to offer. Be brief, upbeat and very clear, and your message will get remembered.

- Remember that most brand new roles, particularly those in small employers, are difficult to find by any other method.

- Even in the public sector people are often tipped off about positions well before they are advertised.

- Be open about what you are doing, but ask for help with research (into sectors and organisations) rather than asking for vacancies.

- Begin with contacts made in your last job, and anyone with professional experience in your circle of family and friends.

- Have a good CV to hand in case you are asked for it, but otherwise don't ask directly for CV advice or job leads – the indirect approach works better.

- Find ways of reaching decision makers when they may have a problem or an opportunity. Good research will help.

- Your last question should always be to ask for recommendations of other people to talk to.

- Remember other spin-offs: word of mouth is the primary method by which candidates get recommended to headhunters and many employers.

- Remember you can also ask for the names of recommended recruitment consultants.

Getting remembered isn't a matter of chance – it's about you planting an idea.

9

Understanding the new rules of work

The rapidly changing world of work has redefined what a 'job' means, and has never before offered such a wide range of ways of working.

If you're looking for work experience you might try temporary or contract work, covering maternity leave, seasonal work, or even a period where you undertake unpaid work. If you want to gain experience and give something back to society you may want to volunteer some of your time, or work as a trustee or in a similar role.

Where you are more experienced and have specialist skills you might consider freelance assignments (projects from a number of organisations), consultancy or project work undertaken on a day rate, or working as an Interim Manager. Senior staff now often move into 'portfolio' careers, mixing consultancy work, freelance projects, retained appointments and Non-Executive Directorships.

- Don't make your preferred working method the main item on your wish list. Demanding particular hours in advance gives employers an early reason to say 'no'.

- If location, travel or flexible working are high up your agenda, they are not to an employer. Keep your powder dry – don't deal with these issues in detail until a job offer is on the table.

- Major on what you have to offer, and what the employer needs. Do your homework on the organisation thoroughly, and ask a lot of questions about current needs and future plans.

- Interrogate openings as problems, not as jobs. Agree what problems need to be solved by an organisation, then talk about the best ways of fixing them.

- Using this approach you may turn a project into a full-time job opportunity, or if you are not looking for a long-term position you may be able to identify a short-term project.

- Listen to others' experience before committing to a new lifestyle. Talk to people working the way you'd like to and find out how they set things up.

- Don't be put off by the record-keeping aspects of self-employment and freelancing – it's simpler than you might think.

- Use social networking sites to expand your contact list and to broadcast a key summary of what you are looking for.

- Don't take a job which adds nothing to your CV, just because it's a job. It's far more useful to you (a) if you can learn something useful or (b) it significantly improves your contacts in a particular field.
- Volunteering can increase your connections and visibility – and it shows that you are keen to remain active.

Work has changed. It's about short-term 'deals', not long-term security.

10

Don't follow the herd

Think for a moment of the actions you could take to ensure that you don't get a new job. One sure-fire way of delaying a positive result is to follow the herd.

The best way to do that is to pursue only advertised jobs. This advice confuses many career changers. Yes, do follow up on interesting job ads, but make that just one part of the mix. Filling in application forms and firing out CVs in response feels like activity, but it's still relatively passive to respond only to things that happen to be out there. Applying only for advertised positions is a safe way of prolonging the agony, as is chasing jobs in declining industries. When you are up against 400–500 others it's usually luck, not technique, that gets you an interview.

A lacklustre job search will give you average results. In ordinary times this will be enough to find you something, but in a 'no excuses' market it guarantees that you'll stay on the shelf – for reasons of your own making.

- Top tip for failure: stay at home in your slippers and cardigan logging on to job sites all day. It will prolong your job search almost indefinitely by keeping you away from real conversations.

- Talk to people – all the time. Start by finding out more about sectors you'd love to work in, and then identify people who are doing the job, and people who hire them.

- Tell friends, relatives and former colleagues what you're looking for, not how difficult life feels.

- Rehearse short, upbeat summaries of what you have to offer and what you're looking for – keep it broad rather than getting bogged down in job titles.

- Keep being curious and interested – employers respond to enthusiasm as strongly as they do to experience.

- Interrogate job ads – look for ideas, information and contacts as well as vacancies.

- Use the Internet to perform in-depth research, not as an excuse to avoid being seen during daylight hours.

- Find trailblazers – people who have already got to where you want to be. Learn short cuts from their experiences.

- Look for organisations that are swimming against the tide, or niche sectors that are doing well.

- Don't use job search as a rehearsal. Get feedback on your CV and interview skills long before you go anywhere near a decision maker.
- Make each employer you talk to feel like your perfect choice – and be ready to say why they should choose you over other equally qualified candidates.

An effective job search means doing *everything* in top gear. Create useful conversations rather than waiting for them to come along.

11

Getting past the age barrier

It may be tempting to link your lack of success in the job market to your age. If you do, remember that the most vulnerable people in the job market are the very youngest, not older workers with experience and connections. However, it remains true that workers over 50 sometimes find that they are rejected in favour of younger workers, despite supportive legislation. Even though we're all working longer, older workers can often face prejudice based on their date of birth.

Older workers who receive repeated rejections are often saying the wrong things – failing to talk about recent experience, constantly talking about out-of-date systems or processes, and constantly making reference to their age. Older workers who are successful are much better at focusing on their strong suits – knowledge, maturity and reliability.

- Don't be put off by bad news stories in the press about older workers. These stories get written even when jobs are abundant.
- Don't draw attention to your age – by giving emphasis to the year you started work, or the year you qualified.
- For the same reason, it's generally not a good idea to refer to the ages of your adult children (they may be older than the person interviewing you).
- Avoid mentioning out-of-date terminology. You were proud of it at the time, but it means as much to today's recruiters as old money.
- Similarly, take the emphasis off any names of organisations, which no longer exist.
- Make your CV focus on what you have achieved and what you have to offer, not on your age.
- Include an email address. Employers often assume that older workers are not IT literate.
- Remember that employers buy experience. Demonstrate how your know-how and maturity will be a benefit.
- Indicate your flexibility and provide recent evidence of your willingness to learn new skills and procedures.
- Try not to reminisce ('in my day . . .') or voice doubts about the wisdom of the current generation of managers.
- Talk about your interest in the work in hand, and

show that you have undertaken a considerable amount of research.

■ Explore the possibilities of mixing and matching different work patterns, including contract and temporary employment.

■ Don't apologise for your age, go on about it, or ask for special consideration.

■ Don't convey a lack of recent relevant experience, but find useful evidence of recent activity, even if it's voluntary work or pursuing your own interests.

■ Demonstrate an active interest in new technology and new ways of working.

Your age will get in the way – but only if you place it centre stage.

SECTION THREE
Your message to the marketplace

12

Getting your message right first time

What happens when someone says to you at a party 'What are you looking for, ideally?' You might begin by talking about job loss. You might answer with a long-winded explanation about the difficulties of the job market or stories of job search setbacks. Your depressing job search history is what you become remembered for.

Then perhaps you mention a couple of job titles – things you're looking for. This doesn't move you forward much either. Most people don't have access to job vacancies, and even if they do they probably don't know you well enough at this stage to recommend you. What's more, job titles mean different things in different contexts.

What you need is a short, memorable package of information which sounds positive *and* gets you remembered.

Learn how to get your message across in two breaths. Something that sums up who you are and where you want to get to. Try two phrases like this:

'I want to do a job that allows me to do A and B and C in an organisation that's doing X and Y and Z.'

A, B and C are the skills you perform well and with energy. X, Y and Z describe the key ingredients in the mix as far as your next employer is concerned – the style, size, culture of the organisation and the outcomes it achieves. You might also talk about the preferred nature of the organisation (private, public, blue chip, privately owned . . .).

Employers, recruitment consultants and networking contacts respond well to this kind of message because it is clear, succinct, memorable and packed with enthusiasm. Listeners hear a set of ingredients that hasn't yet formed into a recipe. They often say things like 'You really should talk to . . .' or 'Have you thought about . . .?' and they name an organisation, a sector or a person.

■ You will use a lot of words looking for a job – in letters, application forms, CVs and interviews. Only a small proportion of them really make a difference.

■ Of the hundreds of words used in your CV or

when you are talking about yourself, how many of them make an impact?

■ Your message needs to be like a radio advertisement – short, focused, and capable of attracting the attention of busy working people.

■ Learn *matching* – adapting your message to different audiences and sectors.

■ Adapt your message into a succinct summary of your wish list in a form you could use with recruitment consultants.

■ Similarly, have a two-breath response to the killer interview question 'Tell us about yourself'.

■ Have a range of focused achievement examples ready for more probing questions.

■ Investigate your choices by talking to people, discovering what's out there. Keep asking the question 'Who else should I be talking to?'

Don't just say it, show it. Talk with enthusiasm – that will get remembered even if the content of your message is forgotten.

13

Cover letters matter

Too many job search attempts collapse at the first hurdle – the cover letter. Sending out a high quality CV beneath a shabby letter – whether it's email or hard copy – is like sending someone a bouquet of roses wrapped in old newspaper.

Your opening salvo of information can make all the difference in terms of shortlisting.

Read the job advertisement and job description carefully. Highlight what you feel are the employer's 4 or 5 'must-have' requirements. In your letter, using bullet points, list 4 or 5 of your matching achievements.

It's a cover letter, not your life story. Avoid excessive detail or working too hard to persuade. Keep it short, focused and very well presented. All it should do is persuade someone that (1) you are very focused on the job, and (2) there is strong enough evidence to bring you in for interview.

- Find out whose desk your letter will land on and address it to that decision maker, not 'Dear Sir/ Madam'.

- Refer clearly to the job title, and vacancy reference number if there is one.

- Send your letter by email and by post – the posted version is likely to be the only one which prints as nicely as you'd like.

- Include clear, unfussy contact details, including an email address you check regularly. If the address on your letter is not within commuting distance of the employer, indicate your willingness to relocate.

- Don't rehearse all the reasons why an employer should be interested in you. Refer again to the employer's shopping list, and make sure you can match each item.

- Don't repeat exact phrases used in your CV: rephrase.

- Don't try to get your personality or sense of humour across in a cover letter. Save it for the interview.

- Avoid beginning every paragraph with the word 'I'. Try to make your letter say as much about the employer as it says about you.

- State why you are attracted to the employer and how you came across the role.

- Use your letter as an opportunity to explain why your skills and experience might be useful, if this is not clear from your CV.

- Your letter will be read by a busy recruiter. Make it interesting and readable, conveying enthusiasm.

- You may use your letter to address significant barriers. If you do not have the relevant qualifications required, you may want to argue the case that your experience provides you with the skills and know-how to do the job.

- Proof-read your cover letter for accuracy as diligently as you read your CV.

- If submitting your CV online it may be simpler to make your email message itself into a covering letter.

Cover letters matter – make yours count.

14

Don't rewrite your CV, rethink it

Too many CVs make only weak connections to the job and many fail to say anything distinctive. Many give out conflicting messages or say nothing at all. Worse still, your CV may be keeping you in a rut.

If you find you're being offered the same tired old jobs you're trying to escape, you are probably responsible. Look at the first 20 words. If you've used limiting job titles or qualifications in the opening section, you'll keep getting pigeon-holed. If you want to change career, you probably need an opening profile that pretty much says what you would say if you were handing the document over to someone in person.

Too many profiles oversell candidates, are full of empty adjectives, and make claims not supported by evidence. By giving your CV 30 minutes' attention, you can avoid that trap.

- Remember that the average reader comes to some kind of decision about you in the first 15–20 seconds of reading your CV.

- Don't write your CV back to front – personal information, details of qualifications and out-of-date skills and job information should not be your lead items.

- Think carefully about the opening words. If you start with 'purchasing professional' or 'languages graduate', you may have put yourself into a category you can't escape.

- Avoid wasting time on the obvious – offering no additional insights beyond what the general reader could guess from your list of job titles.

- Write your profile after writing the whole of your CV. Try to speak it aloud first – it will read more naturally and be more concise.

- A good profile is usually no more than 4 or 5 sentences long to avoid getting over-complicated. The **YOU/ WHAT/ NEXT** model provides a useful structure:

  a) Who are **YOU**, in terms of occupational background, experience, and sector knowledge? Find a summary statement that opens the conversation rather than closing down options.

  b) **WHAT** do you have to offer in terms of know-how and ability, and what have you achieved?

Indicate what in your mix of skills and experience makes you distinctive.

c) What's **NEXT**? This might be a target job statement or an indication of what would be the right ingredients in your next role.

■ Put the strongest statement at the beginning of each paragraph, and the strongest bullet point at the top of each list – there is no guarantee that the reader's eye will go deeper than the first sentence of each block of text.

■ Present yourself in the best possible light, in a credible way that sits within the parameters of checkable history. Stick to the facts as far as dates, job titles and sales figures are concerned.

Page 1 of your CV is a one-page advertisement selling you to a busy customer.

15

Why CVs get ignored

Most CVs are written back to front, with winning messages hidden away or absent, and distracting or irrelevant information offered in the opening moments where the reader gives maximum attention.

Focus on your big-ticket items (skills, specialisms, knowledge of systems, measurable achievements) and promote them in the first 60% of your opening page. After that point the average recruiter has already decided whether or not to give you the green light.

If you don't want a repeat of your last few jobs, you need to sell the idea of change – just as if you were in the room providing some comments before you hand the document over. A new direction usually requires a short profile explaining what you have done, what you have to offer, and where you want to go next. You will probably also want to bring forward details of transferable skills to page 1.

Ways to avoid your CV going straight into the shredder:

- Write your first draft CV in relation to a particular, real job. You will find that this helps you to be focused rather than cataloguing everything.
- Don't write 'Curriculum Vitae' at the top – it makes the document look very old-fashioned.
- Don't include a photograph, your date of birth, or excessive personal information or details of irrelevant jobs you did more than 15 years ago.
- If you're not entirely new to the jobs game, consider leaving out 'interests' unless you can offer something relevant or memorable.
- Make sure that your CV includes all of the relevant keywords or phrases that would be flagged up if your CV text were being searched electronically.
- Try to offer short, uncomplicated explanations for any gaps in your CV.
- Keep your CV to 2 or 3 pages, but remember that page 1 is the one that matters.
- Use strong, one-word active verbs (e.g. *researched*, *organised, created, initiated, led, changed, transformed, built, shaped, influenced*).
- Avoid weak inactive verbs and phrases (*took part in, participated in, contributed to, helped to manage . . .*).

- Don't put yourself down or try irony or humour. It rarely reads the way you want it to.

- Be accurate and honest about dates, job titles and qualifications.

- Don't use fancy layouts, a binder or coloured paper, or laminate your CV.

- Don't try to squeeze too much information on to one page using a small font size or narrow margins – edit instead.

- Communicate in the simplest language you can. Short words and phrases work.

- Don't include the names of referees – provide them separately if requested.

- Don't refer to salary – received or hoped-for. If you are asked for this information, provide it in a covering letter.

- Make sure that the most important points in your CV stand out clearly, just as you would expect key messages to stand out in any form of published advertisement.

CVs are like TV adverts – most are viewed with 25% attention or on fast-forward.

16

Make your job applications more effective

Every tool you use when applying for jobs offers the opportunity to use words – too many of them. Any point of contact with a recruiter or employer gives you a very brief window to get in the 'probable yes', 'maybe' or 'no' piles. In tough times 'maybe' effectively means 'no'.

Most shortlisting decisions are quick-fire and not particularly attentive to detail, so it pays to focus on your key messages. Always condense. Think about what you could say in less than 3 minutes about your background, your history, your target job, or reasons why you match a role.

Opening moments matter – the opening two sentences of your CV or cover letter, or the first words you speak in a telephone conversation or meeting.

Practise openings so you sound natural, positive and convincing.

- Talk to a friend about the things you would say when you get your 3-minute window in front of a recruiter. Make sure that that information heads up page 1 of your CV.

- Adapt your evidence and the language you use to match roles and organisations.

- Write in short sentences or bullet points. Vary their length to make the document easy to read.

- If in doubt, cut, edit and rephrase to make your message as clear as possible.

- Place keywords on the left-hand side of the page, where the reader is more likely to see them.

- Write about relevant interests outside work. Include details of voluntary posts, community roles, work placements, temporary or contract jobs if they communicate evidence of skills.

- Be accurate and honest about dates, job titles and qualifications. Offer short, uncomplicated explanations for any gaps.

- Don't use obscure abbreviations, acronyms or jargon.

- Express what you have achieved in measurable terms – just doing this will often make your CV stand out from the crowd.

- Don't apologise for your CV, qualifications or experience.

■ Use a clear, simple layout in your CV with plenty of white space. Don't include a photograph, the names of referees or details of your current salary.

■ If you start your CV with a profile, keep it free of empty adjectives ('self-starter', 'highly motivated') – particularly if they're the tired phrases used in 90% of documents.

■ If you're completing an application form maximise the benefit of the information you put in each section, and take the opportunity in any space asking for 'supporting information' to sell the 5 main reasons why you should be shortlisted.

■ Edit material by asking the question 'So what?' against every phrase. If everyone else at your level offers the same skill or quality, rephrase or cut.

Selling yourself on paper takes time but gets you in front of decision makers.

SECTION FOUR
Interview secrets

17

Interview success – opening moments matter

When interviews are thin on the ground, it pays to make the most of them.

First impressions matter. Psychologists will tell you that every interviewer makes some kind of decision in the first 30 seconds of an interview, based on the way you dress, sound and act. Try to look the part: when you arrive at reception, check in your coat, bag, umbrella and any other outdoor props. Just take in a slim folder containing the documents you need – that way you look like you already work there.

The initial impression you create will be cross-checked against what you actually say. Again, the first words you say about yourself and your career are remembered more than anything else during the interview.

- Use any chance you get to chat with reception or security staff – it's a good opportunity to warm yourself up for the real thing and you may discover some useful background about the company.

- If you meet people from the team you may be joining, ask useful questions – they may be asked how they feel about you.

- Wear smart shoes and clothes, but break them in beforehand – you should look at ease with yourself.

- Find out in advance who will be interviewing you and their role in the organisation.

- If you have mentioned any out of work interests in your CV, be prepared for an opening question on this topic.

- Don't ignore small talk – it may be taken as a reflection of your ability to make relationships quickly.

- Otherwise, be ready to jump in early on with a detailed discussion of any of the big 5 interview areas: your skills, your achievements, your career ambitions, your knowledge or your personality.

- Avoid getting into secondary areas of discussion (salary, hours, relocation, pension) until as late in the process as possible. Ideally wait until the job is offered.

- Watch for opportunities to demonstrate that you have done your homework on the organisation. A lack of interest in the employer is one of the most common reasons candidates don't get beyond first base.

- If you're offered a drink, don't take it if you shake when you're nervous. You will end up wearing it, not drinking it.

- If you're the kind of person who takes a while to warm up during an interview, ring a good friend 15 minutes before you go in, and rant enthusiastically down the phone about why you want the job. That way you'll begin the actual interview in a much higher gear.

- If there's a glaring gap between your experience and the job criteria, don't stay silent and hope it won't come up. Raise the issue yourself, along with a pre-prepared explanation of why you have compensating experience.

Don't use live interviews as rehearsals – practise and prepare.

18

Standing square to interview questions

Even the shortest contact with the interview process will have shown you that it isn't always the best person who gets the job – it's often the best interview performance. Why put a huge effort into getting short-listed and then fall at the final hurdle?

Don't make the mistake of believing you can 'wing it'. The best improvisations are carefully planned – you need to have a wealth of evidence at your fingertips readily packaged in short, positive bursts of information.

Finally, learn that less is more. Most candidates say too much at interview, and recruiters tune out quickly, then tune back in when you say something negative about yourself or a previous employer.

■ Draw up a very clear checklist before you go into the interview – what is on the employer's wish list, and how do you match it?

- Review your CV – what in it has attracted the employer? Review your achievement stories.

- Rehearse short answers to get round interview questions on delicate subjects like 'Why are you looking for a job right now?'

- Learn 30-second statements using your own words to cover key issues such as your reasons for leaving your last job, your strengths and weaknesses, gaps in your history or qualifications.

- Remember that interview success is about delivering convincing evidence in short bursts. Give a good example, then shut up – the interviewer can then either probe or move on to another item on the checklist.

- Be prepared for the clichés – 'Tell us about yourself', questions on your strengths and weaknesses, 'Where do you want to be in five years' time?'

- If you've got through to interview that probably means everyone on the shortlist can do the job. The key issue then is 'Why you?' Prepare evidence about what makes you different.

- Second interviews are usually not about capability but about whether you fit into the team – watch out for probes on personality issues and your working style.

- Don't be put off by psychometric testing. Ask which tests will be used and do your homework, taking online examples of the test in advance.

- Have two or three smart questions ready for the end – ask about future changes in the role or the organisation.
- Ask for feedback afterwards, but only to improve your performance – it's rare you are told the actual reason why you didn't get the job.

Being shortlisted means the job is in your sights – as long as you don't talk yourself out of it.

19

Communicating the best version of you

Job changers make the mistake of believing they have to pretend to be somebody else – someone more talented. You don't. But you *do* need to present a picture of *you on a good day*. That's why it's important to focus on energy and enthusiasm, even when you are networking. Don't talk about the tough market, talk about the interesting things you've seen and done.

A great way to communicate energy is to talk about highlight events – times when you felt good about your work *and* you made an impact. It's very common for people to be poor at spotting their own achievements, and in British culture we are often reluctant to point to our own successes. Failure to do so may push you off a shortlist.

Learn memorable mini-narratives. Keep them short, focused and entertaining.

How do you recognise your achievements? Here are some tips:

- Look for times when you faced a problem, a challenge, or obstacles. You found some strategy for dealing with the problem – you sought help, or you learned something, or you drew on inner resources.

- Find times when you made a personal contribution. If you were part of a team, concentrate on what *you* added individually. Record the results – look for examples where something clearly changed.

- Try asking your colleagues and friends what differences you have made to roles, and what you have added to organisations.

- Go back through your work diaries and logs. Pick out occasions or projects where you feel you made a difference.

- Don't neglect to search your learning history for examples of times when you overcame difficulties.

- Look at the Job Description for your last job. In what ways did you redefine the job? When have you delivered above expectation?

- Look for times when you invented a new solution or way of working, or rewrote the rulebook.

- Think of times when you went the extra mile, gave extraordinary customer service or brought in new contacts or customers.

- Identify moments when you snatched victory from the jaws of failure.
- Remember to look at achievements in your non-working life. It's often here that you find skills that are undervalued or undeveloped.
- Spot the times when activities would have failed/ lost money/ faded away if you had not been there.
- Try to express some of your achievements in measurable terms. If this is impossible, find the language that conveys other kinds of achievement (e.g. winning people over, communicating an argument, solving relationship problems).
- From the range of evidence available, pick out the ones that will matter most to your target employer and make them prominent in your CV.

Back up any claims you make about yourself with hard evidence from your past.

20

Being memorable

A recruiter friend interviews 6 candidates a day. Driving home he asks himself 'How many can I remember?' The answer? – Rarely more than 2. Most candidates fail to make an impact.

Getting remembered is a key part of the process because breakthrough often comes when your name crops up in someone else's conversation. The mistake is to believe that's a matter of chance. Far more likely, it's something you have chosen to do – an action you've taken which helps you to be, and stay, memorable.

We're not talking about novelty or gimmicks here. We're talking about simple things like strong examples, clarity and originality. Interestingly enough, people who are remembered often have distinctive backgrounds (an unusual out of work interest, a past which includes a colourful career break or a stretch of voluntary work can be enough to make a lasting impression).

- Look again at your CV. How much of it is chopped up job descriptions, and how much is about you?

- What information can you bring forward on to page 1 that makes you distinctive?

- When writing about your skills and achievements, try not to edit old text, but start afresh by looking again at your work history.

- Write down a completely unedited list of every-thing important you have done and learned. Get help from a colleague to edit this material so it will catch someone's attention.

- Where you list an interest in your CV, make sure you can, if asked, say something entertaining on the topic. Better still, write down something that makes you stand out.

- Include in your CV the names of interesting organisations, projects or people you have worked with in the past.

- Interrogate past learning. Don't just list qualifications, say something about what fascinated you.

- Get feedback from any friends or colleagues with interview experience. Get them to interview you for just 9 minutes and practise 3-minute answers to the questions 'Tell me about yourself', 'What do you have to offer?', and 'Why should we choose you?'

- If your answers sound good, make sure they are communicated somewhere in the first half page of your CV.

- Review what you say in any social or work context when somebody says 'Tell us about you'. How quickly do people tune out? How much of your evidence is memorable?

- Remember above all else that what you do affects how long you are remembered. An email and attachment can be ignored, or forgotten in 5 minutes. We can forget a telephone call in an hour or two. A good, face-to-face meeting (ideally followed up with a thank-you note) can be remembered for 6 months. You do the maths.

Being remembered isn't a chance event, it's something you organise from day one of your job search.

SECTION FIVE
Looking forward

21

Your 40-day plan to networking breakthrough

The only sure-fire job search strategy in tough times is to talk to people. Networking can feel wrong – demeaning or exploitative – and it's accompanied by a fear of rejection. If you're shy or reluctant, keep talking to people you know until you gain the confidence to break into a new circle. Put some old misconceptions to rest: it isn't about begging for a job, exploiting everyone you know, or being part of a closed club. It's about the help you ask for in an honest and straightforward manner.

The good news is that it requires a skill set you can learn, and it will put you in touch with likeminded people. In 40 days you can expand your contacts and seriously improve your visibility in the hidden market.

- If success was about the people you already know, there would be little point to networking. It's about expanding your horizons.

- Networking is something we all do unconsciously. If you move to a new town and want to find a good dentist or the best local greengrocer, you will ask people, casually. We learn, share and network all the time.

- Your network as a career changer is going to be focused on people who can give you key information about what jobs are like, how companies are changing, and what trends are affecting your chosen sector.

- Begin with your close circle of friends, and then spread out to professional contacts, clients, suppliers, professional bodies, trade bodies – the list is endless.

- Avoid going in cold. Always start with people you know and then ask them to make the introduction so you never have to begin a phone call 'You don't know me, but . . . '

- Ask people for things they can deliver – for information, not jobs.

- The conversation isn't about you, but about the person you're talking to.

- Find people who can give you up-to-date information about particular sectors. Ask about how people get into this line of work, how the sector is changing, and what makes a top performer.

- Be open about the fact you are looking for names and connections. Ask for the names of other people who can also help.

- Be brief, focused, but try wherever possible to get face-to-face meetings. You will learn ten times more, and you'll be remembered.

- Build slowly, and methodically. Put time aside for the task each week.

- Keep good records. Make a note of the factors that you have in common with your contacts.

- Try to tap into existing networks: interest groups, Internet chat groups, professional bodies, branch meetings . . .

- Think of yourself as a provider as well as a gatherer. Set up an online interest group, circulate information, and pass on the details of the jobs you will fall across. A true network is about co-operation, not competition.

Networking is about research, not job search.

22

Getting unstuck

There are often a number of negative moments in a job search: not getting short-listed, getting turned down after a job interview, or having recruitment consultants fail to return your call.

Repeated rejections and a lack of opportunities may make you feel that the whole process isn't working, or (worse still) you suddenly decide you want to 'lower your sights' in terms of salary or job level. You will probably get absorbed by displacement activities like decorating or gardening, or develop a new interest in daytime TV.

Be careful about adjusting your overall strategy based on a few rejections – few recruitment decisions are logical and transparent. Get someone positive to help you get back on track by revisiting the outcomes that matter to you.

Here are a few strategies career coaches have developed over the years to help you get 'unstuck':

- Anticipate rejection from the outset – you are likely to be rejected for far more jobs and interviews than accepted.

- Set up a support team – a group of people who will encourage new ideas, throw in strategies and support your networking. This is a good time for you to avoid people who describe the glass as half empty rather than half full.

- Once you have spotted an area of work that looks interesting, then it's only a matter of time before paper and screen sources of information don't deliver enough. Conduct more face-to-face research meetings (sometimes known as 'informational interviews').

- Speaking to real people in real jobs is vital: you learn about actual organisations *and* improve your visibility in the hidden job market.

- Remember your successes. Go through your CV again with a supportive friend who can remind you of all the times when you made a difference, and can reinforce your achievements.

- Look for quick wins. Refresh your networking by starting again with people you know well enough to phone without a moment's hesitation.

- Ask yourself how you would undertake this job search if you had been paid to do it for someone else. You would keep providing new ideas and names, not constantly saying 'there's nothing out there'. Stepping out of your narrow perspective prompts new thinking and ideas.

- Talk to pathfinders – people who have made exactly the same kind of career transition as you have. Alumni organisations are particularly useful here.

- Revisit the things you care about most. Look again at the work that motivates you. If it's a field of work you really care about, you will find a way of discovering more.

- Build on synchronicity – connections and opportunities may be just around the corner. Keep pushing on doors – especially the ones that appear to be already open.

Don't stay stuck – get help to see the situation differently.

23

How do I find the *right* role?

Even in tough times, the experience of job instability or redundancy often makes people think about doing a job they will enjoy. It's an idea people struggle with, but in fact, you don't need a job you find satisfying 100% of the time – about $3\frac{1}{2}$ days out of 5 will do the trick – something like a 70% overlap between what the job really needs and those tasks which keep you motivated.

If you're going to put all the time and energy into finding a role that this book suggests, you might as well do something that motivates and interests you, *and* makes an impact as far as an employer is concerned. In fact, this overlap is more likely to get you paid well and promoted in the future.

So forget about getting *any* job – focus on finding the right one – or at least a 'stepping stone' role that gets you where you want to be in the next 12-18 months.

Checklist for working out what types of work would suit you:

- If you disliked your last job, was it the role, your team, the organisation or the field of work you found unappealing?
- What have you enjoyed studying most (academic courses, training events or learning for fun)?
- What would you love to study for its own sake if you didn't need to work?
- What jobs done by friends do you find fascinating?
- Which jobs have attracted you when you saw them advertised, even if you never applied for them?
- What products or services would you feel proud to talk to customers about?
- Of all the jobs you have ever held, which one was the most enjoyable, and why? What assignments or projects did you enjoy in the past?
- What topics do you enjoy talking about with friends?
- What topics do you enjoy reading about (newspapers, magazines, web sites)?
- Think about a time when you had a great day at work. The sort of day where everything went well and you went home feeling a real 'buzz'. Write down what you were doing, what you enjoyed and what you achieved on that day.
- If all jobs paid the same, what work would you do?

- If you could try someone else's job for a day, what would it be?
- If you won the lottery, played with the money for 2 years and then got bored, what would you do to occupy your time?

You spend most of your adult life focused on work – you might as well enjoy it most of the time.

24

Keep your thinking up to date

Generals, we're told, are always 'fighting the last war'. Today's career changers are in danger of using career thinking from the last generation which focused on 'safe' jobs, tried to predict future staff shortages, and was totally unable to predict either the fragility of work today or the range of options available to us.

In normal times, you can wait for something to turn up. In a restricted market, or if you're in a category of people at risk of long-term unemployment, you need to do something else. Responding to panicked advice from family and friends, believing newspaper stories or listening to cynical agency staff will also offer you a scaled-down version of reality. Since there are fewer jobs advertised you will convince yourself that roles don't exist, and miss new opportunities and hidden sectors. You will even use the downturn itself as an excuse to stop looking beyond the obvious, to justify staying in a career rut.

Find good advice, from a range of people. Tired advice fails to reflect what's out there and fails to recognise that we need new career tools for the new economy.

- Don't accept a second-hand or out-of-date picture – get out there and find out for yourself.

- Remember that most of the more interesting roles will never be advertised, particularly in small organisations.

- Don't believe in the picture created by newspaper stories about job losses – new jobs are rarely mentioned.

- Make all your contacts face to face as far as possible – get remembered.

- During the working day, interact with people, not Google. Use the Internet as a research tool, not as your main method of finding jobs.

- Understand that your CV needs to say everything you would say if you were in the room handing it over.

- Don't be put off by tired or cynical recruitment consultants.

- If the market is going downhill, avoid following it with the rest of the herd. Seek niche sectors and organisations that are moving upwards against the trend.

- Don't be frightened by a change of career - it's becoming a necessity for most of us. You may be better off managing the change yourself rather than waiting to be forced.

- Have a strategy for coping with rejection - too many hiring decisions are far too arbitrary to be considered as feedback.

- Admit what you already know - that you are more likely to get your next job through someone you know or meet very soon than through any other method. If you're a betting person, that's where you'd put your money if you were making an educated guess about the most likely success route. So act on that knowledge.

Take control of your career – before somebody else does.

Manage your career for the long term

Extract from
How To Get A Job You'll Love
2009/10 Edition

ISBN: 9780077121808 | PB | Oct-08 | £12.99 | 17.99€

Working Smarter at Your Career

This chapter helps you to:

▌ Understand the importance of planning your career

▌ Explore the way you have made career decisions in the past

▌ Manage 'career blocks'

▌ Invent strategies for coping with personal change

▌ Handle the dark side: deal with the negatives

WHAT IS CAREER MANAGEMENT?

You probably live a life under pressure. You have to juggle priorities and manage your time. Now and again you promise yourself time out to review where you are going, but for most of us change happens when it's forced upon us.

In my work as a careers consultant I say that I specialize in helping people to make difficult career change decisions. The decisions are difficult for a variety of reasons: people don't know what they want to do next, they can't see a way out of where they are now, or they know where they want to be but don't know how to get there.

If you manage your career, actively and consciously, you will make it work better for you. Sometimes this means having a career plan over, say, 5 or 10 years. However, for others, planning ahead is far less important than being *awake* now – awake to the possibilities of change and the urgency of doing work which is more fulfilling and interesting. Those who make conscious decisions about their working lives are more successful and more satisfied. They have thought about the work they want to do and are actively pursuing it. The process has also helped them to understand what kinds of activities outside work are more rewarding. Some have sought out the right job. Others have learned the skill of redesigning the jobs that they do, so that they play to their strengths. You may recognize that your work can be adapted around you so that it is more closely related to your interests or the skills you really enjoy using. Career development doesn't always mean changing jobs.

Career management has many dimensions, including:

▮ discovering the kind of work you find most stimulating and enjoyable

▮ discovering fields of work (including jobs you didn't know existed) where you can make a difference

▮ striking a balance between what you are looking for and what the world has to offer – setting out the steps on your journey

▮ setting goals – these may be financial, learning or personal goals

▮ achieving the right life/work balance – making room for learning, family, relationships, and the things that matter most

▮ making sure that work provides the things that motivate you most – status, recognition, independence, learning, etc.

▮ renegotiating your job so that you can do more of the things that energize you

▮ planning for retirement or changes of lifestyle.

It's worth emphasizing again: if you're looking for boxes to tick, 'to do' checklists, model CVs or letters, look at one of the hundreds of books available that will give you an organized, left-brain solution. We all need good advice when it comes to managing your job search. However, this kind of book works well if you have a clear sense of direction, and all you need is a more effective job search technique. They don't help with the questions many clients express to me: 'Where the **** is my life going?' 'What on earth can I do next?' and perhaps most significantly: 'How do I make the change?'

IS WORK THAT IMPORTANT?

Judging by the amount of time spent complaining about it, it must be. A huge amount of negative energy goes into, and comes out of, work. If it wasn't for work, we would have far less to complain about.

Far too many adults of working age in Europe are either unemployed or underemployed, even in boom times. Being underemployed is as worrying as unemployment: people who are underemployed or in the wrong kind of work become demotivated, depressed or even ill. Work matters.

If we begin with life and work, we should ask ourselves one question: do you **work to live** or **live to work**?

One reason you might **work to live** is that your life's centre is outside your work. You are more motivated by the things you do outside work than the things which earn you a living. You are living out your dream in a different reality, and your salary is there simply to fund your dream. A lot of people live that way, and can be happy. Others feel that something vital is missing, but they struggle to define it.

If you work full-time hours you spend more of your life in work than in any other waking activity (if you live for 70 years, you'll spend about 23 of those years asleep, and 16 years working). Perhaps one reason you're reading this book is because you want more out of that huge slice of life we call *work*.

If you feel that you **live to work**, it may be that you've found the best job in the world. There are dangers here, too: your

109

work/life balance may need adjustment. Perhaps work plays too important a part in your life? Those who suffer the greatest impact of redundancy are those who have made their work the most important thing in their life, perhaps at the expense of family or personal development.

WHAT IS A CAREER?

The idea that we have any choice at all in our careers is a fairly new one. Our great-grandparents' generation believed strongly in the value of hard work, in working your way up to the top, and in the idea of increasing your chances by getting a good education. It's only really since the 1950s that the Western world has grown used to the idea that we make career choices relating to our interests, personality types and backgrounds.

What is a career? To have a 'career' is largely an idea of the twentieth century. Before that, a 'job' was what we would now call an 'assignment' or 'project'; a short-term engagement. People had trades, and were 'jobbing' carpenters, masons, journalists or sailors. A permanent job was one that was attached to an income source arising from an endowment, e.g. a 'living' in a parish church or a royal appointment.

Careers are once again becoming more loose-knit and flexible. Chapter 14 offers you insights into the way you can build a portfolio career.

One definition of the word 'career' is *movement in an uncontrolled direction,* as in 'the steering failed and my car careered across the motorway'. Rapid movement in an uncontrolled direction. Does that sound familiar?

29,000 days

In the past decade the idea of career choice has become closely tied to the idea of *life choices*. In an average lifetime, a woman will live for about 29,000 days (men get rather less, about

110

27,600 days). That's 27,000–29,000 days to learn, work, play, raise a family, leave your mark on life or acquire wisdom. It doesn't sound a lot, does it? Certainly not a lot of days to be saying 'This isn't what I wanted to do when I grew up …'. How you spend those days matters – no matter what your spiritual perspective.

WHAT IS CREATIVE CAREER MANAGEMENT?

Valuing creativity

The first thing to recognize is that we are all capable of inventing extraordinary solutions to cope with life's problems. For most of us these problems are everyday: taking children in opposite directions in one car, paying this week's bills with next week's money, or mending using old bits and pieces rather than buying an expensive component. Sometimes it's the kind of thinking we take for granted, such as taking an engine apart and putting it back together, perfectly, without a diagram, or caring for three or four difficult children at their most unpleasant, or making dinner out of six things found in the cupboard. We are all creative. We have to be: that's how humans have survived.

You will probably have come across many different ways of describing the way people think. However, for many of us lists, plans, diagrams and flowcharts don't work. We don't read life that way. We're inspired by conversations, by people, by movies; our natural creativity needs a different kind of kick-start.

The important thing to remember at this stage is this: we are all given a particular kind of creativity. Career choice is about unlocking what makes *you* a creative, energized person.

There is no point in work unless it absorbs you like an absorbing game.

D.H. Lawrence

What has creativity got to do with career exploration?

We normally use our creative brain to solve problems where ordinary solutions don't work. Isn't your career this kind of problem? You've tried to deal with it logically, by progressing in a sequence from A to Z. You've done the right courses, taken the right initial steps, gained the experience …. Does work provide the right answers? You've tried to look at career change as a business discipline, because you've been told that getting a job *is* a job. Maybe that worked, but did it get you the right job?

We need another method. Every day, business executives wake up and have to think of new ideas: new names for brands, new ways of selling old products, new ways of communicating with people. They have to **generate ideas** on a daily basis. Ideas come from hard work, from experience, but principally from the creative imagination. We all have it. It's the ability to think yourself into someone else's shoes, to think of possibilities, alternative futures, what ifs ….

Where do ideas come from? The age-old question of the tired mind. Writers, designers, inventors and advertising executives all have the same dread: the blank piece of paper. Yet there are ways of learning how to generate ideas. We normally look for the 'right' solution, but creativity works better where we seek multiple solutions: first one idea, then another, then another. Creativity thrives on abundance.

The vital thing is not to confuse idea generating with decision making. How many meetings have you been to where the first good idea is shot down in flames? Ideas are tentative, fragile things that in their early stages can't stand up to the strong light of decision making. It's no use thinking 'I wonder about medicine …' if you immediately say 'Do I want to be a doctor, or don't I?' Forcing a decision too early simply crushes creative thinking. Maybe not a doctor – maybe a medical journalist, or a pharmacist, or a physiotherapist ….

When we think about ideas about our future, we must allow ideas to turn into possibilities, to allow life to be open-ended. That's where this book is designed to help.

When a business enterprise is in decline and heading towards oblivion because it has nothing interesting to offer the market-place, it needs to find a new way of thinking. Right now this business needs some smart thinking: how can it reinvent itself and turn things around? At times like this businesses throw out the rule book and become hungry for ideas that will generate new products and services. If your career is in the doldrums you may benefit from the same kind of thinking: you need to reinvent yourself, rediscover what you are capable of doing and being. As the saying goes, 'if you only live half your life, the other half will haunt you forever'.

Why do people avoid having great jobs?

There are more new jobs out there than ever before, yet at the same time we let our careers be shaped by accident, or accept second or third best because it's easier to stand still than to move forward. Most importantly of all, we insist on using the most limited kind of straight-line thinking in career planning and job search. Why? Essentially, we like to do what feels safe, even if that means being unhappy. There's a powerful part of the brain that says *stop here. It's dull, but it's comfortable. Out there looks difficult and strange.*

And then you find evidence to support your position. You focus on stories of people of your age and background who tried to make a change and failed. I have a theory. At times when change threatens we develop a personal radar that scans the horizon for information. Radar, as you know, is hungry for enemy objects. And we find them. You suddenly discover people who were made redundant and never found a job again. People beat a path to your door to tell you *don't do it … it will all come to tears.*

As you'll discover from reading this book, we come up with all kinds of negative messages to act as blocks to growth and change. If you believe 'I'm not an ideas person' or 'I'm not a leader', your brain is capable of making sure this is a self-fulfilling prophecy. If a golfer says, 'I bet I slice this ball', he probably will.

Adaptability

One of the other reasons that we avoid doing the kind of job we'd love to do is that we are adaptable. Human beings have evolved to become highly adaptable creatures, capable of living in temperatures from −30 to +50°C, and capable of living in the most demanding, unhealthy and difficult conditions. Perhaps because of this in-built survival instinct, some of us have the capacity to do something which modern society finds odd and most of history saw as the norm: to do an unpleasant job for years, or even decades. However, given a world of choice, the fact that we can carry on doing the same old job doesn't mean that we should.

Let's be realistic ...

Applied early in the process of rediscovering your potential, so-called 'realistic' thinking can be deadly, because it's all too often not about what is real but what is acceptable, conventional or safe. How many successful brands or products started life by being conventional? It is true that organizations and people all have constraints: bills to pay, mouths to feed. It's important not to underemphasize that fact. However, what matters is that these basic requirements are seen for what they are, not the centre of life.

Put another way, incremental thinking only gets you incremental results. But if you don't take even the small steps, you can pretty much guarantee that nothing will change at all.

'I just need a job'

By now you may have come to the conclusion that creative career management might be a good thing for somebody else. Why not you? Because you feel that reality is harder and tougher than that. You need something real, right now, that pays the bills. You just need a job. This might be because you're unemployed, or because you're just not paid enough to make ends meet. This places you in a vulnerable position in the labour market. It forces you to become a job beggar, going round with your hat in your hand saying just one thing: I need a job. Desperately.

I spent some time in early 2000 working with a group of job seekers from one of the townships in Johannesburg. One of them, Gugu, was aged 17 and had given up looking for work. Why? 'There are no jobs in South Africa', she said. But new jobs are being created in that country every day … 'Yes, but so many people are chasing them', she said sadly. Talking to her I realized that too many job seekers are giving a totally undifferentiated signal. Fortunately, she and her fellow job seekers all found jobs as a result of a programme which allowed her to focus on her strengths, and gave her the tools to demonstrate them to employers.

No, it's true: I just need a job

Do you really? How long will it be before you're back asking the same questions: What am I doing this for? Where's my life going?

If that's the reality facing you, then don't use it as a justification for suppressing what you have to offer, otherwise you end up saying that there's no point thinking about my career, my skills, my future, because there are no choices. There are very few occasions when that's true. And if you need money, just earn it. Don't pretend that's all there is. We all have choices.

There will always be those who say '*get real* – few of us have the luxury of career choice'. Yet we all know people who broke out of that box. Listen to successful people talking about the work they do. They don't often say 'Well, the money's good'. They talk about work being like a 'game', being 'fun' or 'the best job in the world'; they talk about the privilege of doing for a living what they would gladly do for nothing.

Another interesting fact: people get brilliant jobs even in the depths of recession. For more than a decade the UK has enjoyed low unemployment, and more people have been employed than at any time in its history, yet people still said 'this is a really bad time to be unemployed'.

How many excuses do you need to have to ensure you stay miserable at work?

Effective career planning is about finding a job that works for you, matching who you are to the life you are going to lead. That's not a luxury: that's the clearest reality there is. Doing that provides you with a great career, and gives you a greater chance of contributing to life.

Working smarter rather than harder at career building

It's sometimes said that the right job is out there somewhere looking for you, but you can't sit at home and wait for it to knock on the door. The majority of us have to rely on a mix of good judgement, inspired guesswork and a pinch of luck. Luck has been described as two mathematical laws working together: chance and averaging. We can't control chance, but we can increase the odds in our favour. Invest in your future. Use your precious thinking time carefully, and learn to think openly, because a moment's inspiration can sometimes take you far, far further than a year's dull planning.

Setting objectives is a vital part of the process. Ideas without activity are daydreams. The danger is that we move too quickly

Figure 1.1 Career transition funnels

to activity without really taking the opportunity to reinvent our career. Exploring is an opening-out process. We tend to think along tramlines, moving logically from one stage to the next. Divergent thinking works rather differently. Let your imagination fan out: rather than making decisions too soon, look at possibilities. Try on ideas. Figure 1.1 shows how once you have really worked through the process of idea building, you will reach a point where you have enough information to start setting concrete objectives. At this point the funnel reverses, and you consciously close down options and aim for specific outcomes. This book takes you from the point of exploring to the point of setting real goals.

TAKE A SIDEWAYS LOOK AT CHANGE

People differ in their attitude to change. Some enjoy the energy and challenge of change, but they are often attracted by the next big new idea. Others find change disturbing because it involves moving from the known to the unknown.

Modern society seems to favour those who enjoy the excitement that comes with change. One of the difficulties of this type of person is that they sometimes make a decision based on the most radical or innovative outcome, rather than the best outcome. These **change masters** are often insensitive to the impact of change on others who are less gung-ho about the whole process.

Many people in work **suffer** change. If you feel like this, all you will hear every day is the message that 'the only certainty is the certainty of change'. I hear from fellow careers counsellors of many who feel victimized by the new culture. In a world of 'hot desking' they feel constantly anxious, unsettled – these people would work more productively if they were allowed office space to call their own. Others are fairly responsive to change if they are sold the benefits, but very wary of 'change for change's sake'.

Be experimental

To think 'it's all experimental' is a great approach to life, far better than a blame culture. Experiment and failure, 'making mistakes', is a necessary part of creative thinking. And if you are going to use the word failure, then 'fail forwards' rather than 'fail backwards'; in other words, make your mistakes positive steps forward in your learning. Every successful product brought to market required a thousand near-misses. Experiment away.

No-one can persuade another to change. Each of us guards a gate of change that can only be opened from the inside. We cannot open the gate of another, either by argument or by emotional appeal.

Marilyn Ferguson

Also available from Bestselling Author and Career Coach – John Lees

How To Get A Job You'll Love, 2009/10 Edition
9780077121808 £12.99 PB

John Lees challenges you to rethink what work means to you in his bestselling guide to unlocking your hidden talents and finding your ideal career. *How To Get A Job You'll Love* teaches you how to understand your personality, skills and motivators to identify the type of career you really want. Packed full of practical exercises, checklists and inspiring resources.

Why You? CV Messages To Win Jobs
9780077115104 £9.99 PB

Your CV makes a critical first impression in the competition for a job you'll love. It's not just about what your CV looks like, but what it says and how it communicates a focused message about what you have to offer employers. Based on extensive research that offers fresh insights into the way employers read CVs. This step-by-step guide helps you develop the right format to match your needs and aspirations and effectively use your CV as apart of a multi-strategy job search.

Job Interviews: Top Answers To Tough Questions
9780077119096 £9.99 PB

Got that all important interview soon? This book will put you streets ahead of the competition, helping you think through hundreds of tough questions and respond with total confidence. Whether you are a first time job hunter or going for your dream promotion, this is your comprehensive toolkit for dealing with awkward, probing, personality and competency based interview questions.

Take Control of Your Career
9780077109677 £12.99 PB

Whether you want to advance up the career ladder or make the transition to a more interesting role, or improve your work/life balance, this practical guide gives you the tools and techniques to achieve your goals and develop the best career strategy for you.

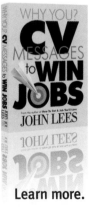
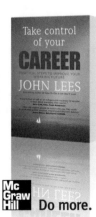

An Opportunity for Career Coaching with John Lees Associates

If you would like to build on the tips outlined in this book, why not consider a career coaching session with one of the team engaged by John Lees Associates?

We specialise in helping people to make difficult career choices. Building on John Lees' successful range of careers books, JLA has engaged a team of Associates in various parts of the UK to provide 1:1 career counselling which will help you to transform your career.

Whether you are changing jobs or interested in developing your career, you need to invest time in making the right decision. Working with one of our consultants, using material tried and tested through books by John Lees, is a great step towards finding work that will match your personal wishlist.

By purchasing this book you are entitled to a 15% discount on your first 2-hour session. Simply quote reference JI2009.

Using the JLA Skill Cards as part of your interview preparation

The New JLA Skill Card sort offers a step-by-step guide to identifying your motivated skills.

Full instructions are provided to enable you to gather evidence of achievement, rehearse focused mini-narratives, and use that evidence in writing a CV or preparing for a job interview.

Simply quote reference JI2009 - Cards to purchase a discounted card sort at a discounted price of £15.00 including postage (normal price £22.00).

Email info@johnleescareers.com to take advantage of either of these special offers.

Learn more. Do more.